GW00578305

Colchester

in old picture postcards

by
George Pluckwell

European Library - Zaltbommel/Netherlands MCMLXXXIV

GB ISBN 90 288 2531 2

European Library in Zaltbommel/Netherlands publishes among other things the following series:

IN OLD PICTURE POSTCARDS *is a series of books which sets out to show what a particular place looked like and what life was like in Victorian and Edwardian times. A book about virtually every town in the United Kingdom is to be published in this series. By the end of this year about 175 different volumes will have appeared. 1,250 books have already been published devoted to the Netherlands with the title* **In oude ansichten.** *In Germany, Austria and Switzerland 500, 60 and 15 books have been published as* **In alten Ansichten;** *in France by the name* **En cartes postales anciennes** *and in Belgium as* **En cartes postales anciennes** *and/or* **In oude prentkaarten** *150 respectively 400 volumes have been published.*

For further particulars about published or forthcoming books, apply to your bookseller or direct to the publisher.

This edition has been printed and bound by Grafisch Bedrijf De Steigerpoort in Zaltbommel/Netherlands.

INTRODUCTION

Colchester is situated in the County of Essex, 51 and ¾ miles from London. It is also not far from the East Coast of England. A few years before the birth of Christ, Colchester – then known as Camulodunum – was governed by Prince Cunobelin, the warlike character who figures in Shakespeare's play 'Cymbeline'. This ambitious Iron Age ruler made Colchester his headquarters; though the site of that ancient city probably covered more ground. Some 14 square miles. Camulodunum was a large and strong promontory fortress. It occupied the crest of a broad ridge of ground lying between the Rivers Colne and Roman. It was thought to be the Capital of Iron Age Britain for Cunobelin was classed by the Romans as the most powerful King in Britain. After a long and very successful reign he died in about the year A.D. 40. A few years later his stronghold capital was invaded by Claudius, the great Roman Emperor, who entered the ancient fortress city of Camulodunum (Colchester) riding on an elephant, although how he got them across the English Channel I can not imagine. He founded the first British Colonia there to be given the names of Victricenses (in honour of the victory) and Claudiana (in honour of himself). Further to cover himself with glory, he decreed that a temple be erected to his deity. In A.D. 61 Boudicca, Queen of a Norfolk tribe, made her revolt against the yoke of Rome. They had made slaves of the British tribes and brave Boudicca, sometimes described as an ancient British Battleaxe, was fighting for justice and freedom. She descended on Camulodunum and the new Colonia and burnt the grand Temple of Claudius to the ground. Later, after a big battle, that stouthearted Queen took poison rather than fall or surrender into enemy hands. She will ever stand for freedom in English history.

Thereafter Colchester was walled in and made safe from future revolts or attacks. It seemed to settle down contentedly under Roman rule for about four hundred years. With many public buildings, baths, outside farms and villas for officers and their families with under floor heating. Today indications of the extent to which Roman civilization predominated are to be found in the Castle Museum, just off the High Street in the fine pleasure area the Castle Park.

So the town, once capitol of Iron Age England, never regained its early importance in the Imperial Roman scheme and became merely a country provincial town.

There is a colourful legend of King Cole, a rich character in Colchester's history. In 238 A.D. Cole, general or governor of this district under Rome, seized the government of those parts now known as Essex and Hertfordshire. In the year 242 his famous daughter Helena was born in the town. Eighteen years later Constantius, the Roman general in Spain, came and besieged Colchester. After the siege was raised he married Helena to whom he had given his heart. A son was born of their happy union, who in due course became Constantine the Great. Helena, a doer of good works, later made a saint travelled to the Holy Land and discovered the Holy Sepulchre and the Cross. There is a statue of Saint Helena on top of Colchester's Victorian Town Hall in the High Street, holding a cross. It was discovered a few years ago that she is in fact not the reputed Saint Helena, but a likeness of the Virgin Mary.

In the ninth century the terrible Danes invaded Colchester with their custom of rape and pillage. Shortly afterwards Edward the Elder came with his West Saxon army and repaired the town walls and the people submitted to him, who before were under the dominion of the dreadful Danes. This opened up a new period in the history of Colchester, marked by its change of name to Colneceaster; the town by the River Colne.

The Norman Conquest in 1066 brought prosperity to Colchester. William's principal liege in Essex was Eudo, the dapifer or high steward. He built the castle on top of the Roman Vaults of Claudiuses ruined temple and founded the Abbey of Saint John. He personally owned five houses and forty acres and half the church of Saint Peter (half its endowments). Bad King John visited the Town on many occasions and after the signing of the Magna Charta attacked the Town in 1216. It led to a sorry state of affairs with the French that the barons had installed to withstand a siege, laying down their arms and soon were under escort to London. While wicked John took the great Castle of Colchester.

They always seemed to have a conflict of somekind in Colchester rich history. For King Henry VIII (of six wives fame) suppressed the wealthy Monasteries in Tudor times and let his favourites plunder the Essex Religious Houses, including Saint John's Abbey in Colchester. During the terrible Civil War, when family fought against family, the Town endured a Great Siege and bravely held out for 76 days, sometimes eating mice, rats, cats and even horses.

In 1648 some Royalists, named Lucas and Lisle, under George Goring Earl of Norwich marched their troops into the Town and declared it to be a Royalist stronghold for King Charles I. The population was mostly in sympathy with Parliament and the Roundheads, Cromwell's General Fairfax quickly surrounded the walled fortress that was Colchester and starved them into surrender. Fairfax firstly offered them a free pardon if they surrendered, but the mighty Headgate was shut and barricaded leaving several hundred Parliamentarian troops inside. The Royalists killed them to a man and the siege continued. The Roundhead General also fined the poor townsfolk £14,000 after the siege. If they did not pay, he said, his soldiers would pillage and plunder the town. The damage to Colchester was great indeed. Hardly a church remains which does not show evidence of having been rebuilt in the early eighteenth century.

As regards trade Edward III had introduced Flemish weavers into Essex and in the fifteenth century a large number of Dutch refugees found their way to Colchester and developed an important industry in the Bay and Say Cloth trade. So important in fact that during the siege they felt emboldened to propose to General Fairfax that he should allow them to come and go between the town and their regular customers. To which he responed by informing them that gentlemen in his camp would pay fair prices for all the stuff they would bring to Lexden Heath (not far outside the town walls). They did not seem to have accepted his offer.

The Romans had a passion for oysters and Colchester fishery is of great age. Richard I confirmed the then existing rights with regard to the fishery from the North Bridge as far as Westnesse. And although the rights have been challenged, they still exist. They also have a Colchester Oyster Feast, held annually in October at the Town Hall or Castle. Members of Parliament, filmstars and other famous personalities, numbering some 400, eat and enjoy as many as 10,000 oysters.

In 1901 the total population was 38,373 and by 1963 it had risen to over 100,000. Some population explosion.

Colchester was one of the largest military centres in the country in 1909 and is still a garrison area with many barracks, with names like Artillery. Some of the Victorian barracks were red brick buildings with stables downstairs for the horses. One imagined the soldiers and their wives lived up stairs in kind of old fashion flats with heavy wrought iron balconies. Conditions were very primitive in those far off Empire days. Just a wooden bed and table screwed to the floor in case of breakages. Candle or perhaps oil lamplight and squares of lino on the well scrubbed floor. (How contrasting to the houses of modern day soldiers.)

Colchester is justly proud of its modern day engineering firms. Some old established like Woods Ltd., who make metal fans, and Paxmans Ltd. for engines and boilers. The modern Town is a thriving place and the old weavers cottages in the Stockwell Streets blend in with the skyscrapper buildings of the Telecom Centre and Insurance office blocks.

So the ancient Town of Colchester today is known for Oysters, Cants Roses, Engines and Colchester United Football Club and Players. Not overlooking the New University of Wivenhoe which Colchester has placed in the Borough. So Colchester still bears that proud title: the oldest recorded town in England and capitol of Iron Age Britain.

My grateful thanks to Mr. Peter Sherry for his great help with the old postcards. And to Mr. Val. Stone for assisting me with this project. To Miss Barbara Cartland, the Novelist, for her faith and encouragement in my writings. Also Colchester Public Library who kindly have given me information.

1. This 1902 scene of Colchester High Street is observed from the junction of North Hill and Head Street before the electric tram era. There is none of the hustle or bustle one now associates with the busy High Street. It even appears rather muddy from the horse-drawn traffic. The large colonnaded building on the left is the Suffolk and Essex Insurance Company offices. In the previous few decades it has been converted into various shops. Next to the Fire Office, as it was often called, are the Albert Hall and Art Gallery. This was once the old Corn Exchange. It has served many purposes including the Towns Repertory Theatre. Further down, still on the left, is the Victoria Clock Tower of the New Town Hall just completed. There was a Hansom Cab Rank outside the impressive Fire Office. This gives the picture true Edwardian flavour.

High Street, Colchester

2. The same scene in 1910. Showing three types of transport and a busier High Street. On the left a proper country pony and trap while near right is a smart early type enclosed saloon motor car. A fine open top electric tram is outside the Fire Office. Trams, then the modern transport, arrived in Colchester in 1904 and lasted until 1929. The High Street runs straight within the Town Walls in true Roman fashion.

High Street, Colchester

3. The High Street in 1903 before the period of the trams. One can behold Jumbo, the giant water tower in the background. It is a well known local landmark and visitors always spot it towering up into the skyline from our Colchester North Railway Station and know that they have arrived at the right town. That and the Victoria clock tower of the Town Hall are unmistakable. There is some curious carriage or coach on the right hand side of this postcard. There once was a small church of Saxon origin, called Saint Runwald, that stood out nearly in the middle of the High Street not far from the Town Hall site. This little church, a fine specimen of the Perpendicular, lay desolate for many years and was unfortunately entirely cleared away in 1878.

High Street, Colchester.

The „IXL" Series.

4. Another High Street view with gas lamps on either side of the picture. The (cream coloured) building on the right with the colourful flower boxes outside is the ancient George Hotel. This former coaching inn goes back to Georgian times and is full of old oak beams and in the cellars there are sections of the historical Roman Town Walls. In days long gone many a hunting party after the sly fox would leave their horses outside and enjoy refreshment at the George. It is still open for trade and customers in this year of grace 1984 and long may it reign (1903).

5. The Renaissance style High Street Town Hall was completed in 1902 at the cost of £62,000. It was designed by Mr. John Belcher and the foundation-stone was laid by the Duke of Cambridge in 1896. This splendid structure was built on the site of the previous Victorian Town Hall, pulled down in 1894 because it was not grand enough. Originally the same site had held the ancient Norman Moot Hall. On the exterior walls are niches containing statues of six famous people prominently associated with the Town's history. Including Samuel Harsnett, Archbishop of York, once son of a Colchester baker, who died in 1544 and bequeathed a valuable collection of books to the Town. The principal apartment is called Moot Hall or Assembly room with a good organ. On top of the Victoria Clock Tower can be seen the supposed figure of Saint Helena and Cross, 160 feet high. Only in truth it is a likeness of the Virgin Mary (the only statue available). Part of the Cup's Hotel can be viewed on the left (1905).

NEW TOWN HALL, COLCHESTER

NORTH HILL, COLCHESTER.

6. North Hill and High Street junction, looking down the Hill from the Head Street direction. On the left is the Waggon and Horses Public House complete with swinging barrel signs and centre lamp. Next to a narrow lane, known as Balkerne Passage which leads to the Roman Balkerne Gateway, is William Simkin, Furnishers and Valuers. While on the right can just be seen the shop premises of A. Halls, Fishmonger, Oyster Catcher and Poultry seller. Behind his shop is the lofty tower of Saint Peter's Church (1920).

7. North Hill before the trams in 1900 was quite a tranquil place and one can see the High Woods in the background down North Hill. One can behold The Waggon and Horses on the left and William Simkin's advertising board jutting out. He was a jack of all trades being also a cabinet and chair maker, upholsterer and even undertaker! While on the right hand side is a good view of Saint Peter's seventeenth century restored Church Tower. It has illuminated dial clock faces, dating from 1866, which jut out over North Hill. Saint Peter's is still open for services.

NORTH HILL, COLCHESTER.

31190

8. This delightful Edwardian picture of 1907 depicts the top of North Hill where it merges or joins High Street and Head Street. The girl in the foreground is probably a grandmother by now. And note the ladies passing the time of day in the shade of Saint Peter's seventeenth century lofty brick church tower. Colchester was originally built on a hill or area of raised ground completely surrounded by Roman and later Norman Town Walls. Further down the steep mountain like North Hill the old cattle market of Middleborough was situated. In recent years the cattle market has completely vanished under the hands of the redevelopers and town planners. North Hill still has much character, a blend of Tudor and Georgian houses with quaint cobbled tiled roofs.

East Hill, Colchester

9. In this study of East Hill, dated 1906, we are looking in the direction of the eastern end of the High Street by the Castle. On the middle left is the Church Tower and Spire of Saint James' and in the far distance one can just make out the Town Hall Clock Tower. There seems to be a heavy waggon rumbling along in the centre of this scene, pulled by two strong carthorses. It is probably a brewer's dray from the East Hill Brewery that can just be seen in the background right. The cottage on the right, with the overhanging gable, would probably have been the previous home of some Flemish or Dutch weaver, who worked in the Bay and Say trade.

10. This 1910 photograph gives one a good idea how the Siege House and East Bridge looked to our forefathers. The Siege House is probably some 450 years old. Its name is not its only memory to the Great Civil War Siege for owing to its position, it suffered a goodly peppering of Royalist bullets and the effects can still be seen plainly today. Marked or ringed in red they are round holes in the outside beams or woodwork. East Bridge can just be seen in the background between the ornamental gas lamps. This bridge spans that section of the River Colne and on the other side is situated Marriages Flour Mill, very well known in Colchester's history. Today that greybrick square tower shaped structure has taken on a new lease of life as a luxury Hotel and Restaurant.

Old Siege House, Colchester

11. The Old Siege House, as already mentioned, was peppered with shot during the Siege of 1648. Later it was owned by Marriages Flour Mill for a number of years and they must have preserved it well. For recently on the closure of the mill it was sold. Now after more renovations, which have not spoilt the Olde Worlde atmosphere, it has opened as a high class Restaurant or Eating house. And is by all accounts a tourist's attraction with beautiful views of swans and boats on the silvery tidal Colne River it almost overlooks. The flour barges have gone for good, with their red and golden sails, but the nearby Hythe riverside district or dockland is still busy with Dutch and German Cargo ships, bringing coal, fish meal and various other cargoes up to the Hythe quays. The Siege House appears unchanging, only its purpose has moved with modern time (1905).

HIGH ST EAST, COLCHESTER.   D.F. & Co York

12. This postcard of 1910, somehow taken at night, reveals the High Street taken from a East Hill angle. One can spot or observe Saint Nicholas' spire and the Town Hall Clock Tower in the distance. The Tudor building with the mullioned windows and bright lamp outside is the very historical Grayfriars, now owned by the Borough Council. (Once it had Franciscan connections.) Perhaps this card was a trick one coloured by hand. I do not think they had suitable camera's for taking night time photographs in those days.

13. This study of Saint Nicholas' Church was taken from what I term the eastern end of the High Street before it disappears down East Hill. Saint Nicholas' was probably named after the original Father Christmas. It was first erected in the twelfth century and named after that patron saint of children. The church was once noted for its projecting clock and quite a few townsfolk referred to the time dial as 'The frying pan' on account of its resemblance to that household utensil. During 1875-76 Saint Nicholas's was completely restored at the cost of £15,000 and the spire was added. The church was unfortunately demolished in 1954 and the ground sold to the Co-operative Society, who soon built a gigantic superstore on the site naming it Saint Nicholas, in memory I suppose (1900).

Colchester Castle, N.W.

14. Colchester Castle is situated in the beautiful Castle Park at the eastern end of the High Street. Tourists might be forgiven for thinking it appears rather like an enlarged version of a child's toy fort. It is really all that remains of the largest Norman keep in England. It was erected in the eleventh century by the powerful Eudo Dapifer, steward of William the Conqueror, who has his statue on a ledge outside the Town Hall. With walls over 12 feet thick and originally twice as high, it measured 155 feet by 113 feet exclusive of projecting buttresses and the chapel apse (1901).

Colchester Castle

15. This view of the front displays the impressive round Norman doorway arch in all its splendour. There are dark Dungeons, Roman Vaults, for the Castle stands on the foundations of Claudiuse's great temple and in the North West Tower even a Norman latrine (toilet). Possibly on account of its strength of position and design, the Castle has been only twice 'under fire'; once in the time of bad King John and again during the great Siege of Colchester in 1648. The Castle is rectangular in structure with towers at the four corners. The general picturesqueness of the exterior of the Castle owes not a little to the charming little turret at the south west corner (1902).

The Castle, Colchester.

16. During the Civil War in 1648 Sir Charles Lucus, Sir George Lisle and Sir Bernard Gascoigne, the Royalist commanders who held Colchester for twelve weeks against the Parliamentary forces, were briefly confined, traditionally in the long vault to the east of the well house. Gascoigne was reprieved, but Lucas and Lisle were shot in the Castle bailey, where an obelisk now commemorates the event. They say no grass will grow on that spot (1902).

Colchester Castle.

17. Some thirty years later the Castle was sold for £110 to a miserable fellow named John Wheely, who dug out some of the Roman Vaults searching for gold or treasure. He did not discover any so started dismantling the upper storeys of the Castle and selling the materials. Wheely was at last forced to acknowledge the superiority of the stout workmanship of the Castle and dismantling became a very unprofitable business. Consequently he sold what was left of the Castle to Sir Isaac Rebow (famous local person). So the Castle entered happier times and after passing to various owners it came into the hands of Captain Charles Round, who opened up a Museum there, begun in 1846 in the crypt. The tree growing on the roof of the tower was a sycamore, traditionally planted by the then Mayors daughter to commemorate the battle of Waterloo (1815). It is still there today. Postcard from 1905.

CASTLE PARK, COLCHESTER

18. The Castle and grounds were bought for £10,000 by the Viscount and the Viscountess of Cowdray. Being kind local benefactors, they presented this splendid possession to the Borough in 1922. They gave many gifts known as the Cowdray Gifts which was their lasting Memorial of The Great War (1914-1918). The Castle was only partly roofed in those days around an open type of quadrangle. It was not completely covered in until 1935. Today they have a Castle Appeal Fund and are hoping and endevouring to raise over half a million pounds to repair and renovate those stout walls, which have seen so much history. They are trying to save our heritage for future generations (1904).

COLCHESTER

River Colne,

19. The River Colne flows through part of Castle Park and on the other side of this bridge, called Middleborough (after the old Cattle Market), there is a public footpath into the Park. The lath and plaster Tudor cottage in the picture was a riverside Café of character for a number of years. It was called the 'Copper Kettle' and had a giant kettle sign hanging outside which was most unusual. This building still survives and the Victorian bridge was altered in 1903 to make it wider for the new Borough trams which routed the Town in 1904 (1910).

The Castle Park, Colchester

20. Castle Park is a good recreational place and not a stones-throw away from the busy traffic filled High Street. The Park which extends from the Castle and sweeps down to the River Colne and beyond. Between the Monument to the shot or executed Royalist officers and the massive Castle is a shady avenue of trees known as The Mayors Walk. Due from the circumstance that the trees were planted in 1892 by the Lord Mayor of London and Mayors of Colchester, Ipswich and Harwich and seven other towns (1905).

Castle Park, Colchester.

21. A 1903 postcard of Castle Park overlooking the River Colne. Behind the Castle is the ramparts and near the ornate Bandstand (which it still there), they did some excavations in 1920. Amazingly they discovered the remains of a whole street of Roman houses. Boudicca was thought to have burnt them down in her Great Revolt, because they discovered charred remains in the the ruins.

Colchester Pageant
Roman Soldiers

22. The Edwardians were very fond of open air pageants and had a Colchester one nearly every year from 1904. Adults and children enjoyed dressing up and reacting their glorious local past. In this scene the Roman soldiers seem to be attacking the white clad figures in the background of Castle Park. Perhaps they were the ancient Britains (1909).

Colchester Pageant
Osyth and her Nuns with Priest

23. This is the panorama of Saint Osyth and her Nuns, dated 1904. Saint Osyth is a local Essex figure and her tale is a very strange one to relate. The raiding Danes cut off her head and she walked carrying it to the Church of Chick where her martyrdom was miraculously marked for all time by the sudden appearance of a spring of clear water. Which can still be seen in the north-west corner of Saint Osyth's Priory grounds in a section known as the Nuns Wood.

COLCHESTER

24. This postcard has an unusual story to recount. It was bought in Colchester by an English person who journeyed to Brussels in Belgium, and then sent or posted to someone, probably a friend or relation, in Rowhedge, two miles from Colchester. It shows a nice view of the lake in Castle Park with typical English swans (1910).

Cricket Pavilion, Castle Park, Colchester.

25. Colchester's Castle Park has always encouraged the sporting side of life and this charming study of the Cricket Pavilion, taken in 1911, proves that point. In the Town Guide of that period it states *Colchester and East Essex Cricket Club have a good ground in Castle Park which is visited by the County Club during the annual Cricket week.* Tennis was also played in the courts there.

CASTLE PARK, COLCHESTER.

all well. Your dear friend Mrs P... is quite well thought you would like to...

26. The lower Castle Park was open to the public in 1893 and the lake on the left was then still unfinished. Middle Mill is shown on the extreme left behind the trees by the River Colne which twists through the Park. Military Bands played fortnightly for the entertainment of the townsfolk for many years (1903).

27. This unique view of High Street was taken in 1899 when Queen Victoria still sat on the throne. We are looking in the eastern direction towards East Hill. It is a fine picture of Saint Nicholas' Church which then dominated the Townscape for the Town Hall was still being built. The high building on the front right hand side is the venerable Tudor Red Lion Hotel. This was another old coaching inn like the George and is still very much open for business today. Note the beams have been plastered over on the frontage. They were exposed again at a later date. The shops next-door but one are now a big modern Woolworth's Superstore. The cobble stones in the foreground of the picture mark the spot called Middle Row. Where Saint Runwald's Church and tiny shop stood out almost in the middle of the High Street. All was cleared away by 1878.

High Street, Colchester.

8178.   4.

28. Colchester High Street in 1913, looking towards the Head Street and North Hill junction. The white building behind the gas lamp-post on the right is Mann's Music Shop and near-by is the tall structure of the Lamb Hotel, followed by the Hippodrome Theatre and the Town Hall. While on the left, by the carriage, is the historic Red Lion Hotel. The tramlines denote the era of the Borough electric trams that routed the Town until 1929. Covering East Gates, Hythe, Lexden, and North Station. Also Recreation grounds.

HIGH ST LOOKING WEST, COLCHESTER.

29. Colchester High Street in 1905 was vastly contrasting from the previous era or scene. Trams were the kings of the road. The flags and banners decorating the High Street were probably for the yearly pageant held in Castle Park. There is a good view of the George Hotel, once a coaching inn, on the right. The Town Hall now dominates this section of the High Street like Big Ben and the Houses of Parliament in London. It would become a very familiar town landmark to local people.

30. The Public Library in West Stockwell Street in the old Dutch Quarter of Colchester was the first of its kind here. It was built in 1894 on a foundation bequest of £1,000, left in 1890 by Robert Catchpool to start a Public Library. This Victorian mock Gothic style structure has a certain grace and character. The Library later moved to Shewell Road in the centre of Town and eventually quite recently to its modern building in Trinity Square. Famous authors, like Defoe of 'Robinson Crusoe', visited Colchester. Defoe looked at the massive Castle and remarked 'It has not fallen yet, nor will another 120 years, I believe, make it look one jot older.' (1899.)

TUDOR HOUSES, STOCKWELL ST. COLCHESTER.

31. Tudor Houses in the Stockwell area of Colchester. There are two Stockwell Streets East and West situated between the Town Hall and Castle Park location or district. This old Dutch Quarter, as it is called, is associated with the sixteenth century Flemish and Dutch refugees who set up a woollen industry there. The most important of these light woollen type of serge fabrics was the 'Bay or Say'. Today it is a well preserved attractive tourists attraction.

32. In 1884 there was a startling earthquake in Essex. This was severely felt in the district between Colchester and the Blackwater. Damage shown here is to houses in the Stockwell Street vicinity (Old Dutch Quarter). It was the worse of its kind in the British Isles for about four centuries. Among the 1,200 buildings damaged in the neighbourhood were 20 churches and 11 chapels (1884).

33. This picture shows more devastation by the earthquake in the Old Dutch Quarter. The Lord Mayor of London set up a Mansion House Relief Fund and over 8,906 pounds were subscribed and distributed among 381 private owners who required help for restoration of their property. They say Queen Victoria was so touched at Her subjects sad plight that Her Majesty donated a goodly sum to get the Relief Fund started (1884).

34. Postcard makers could occasionally muddle things up and give wrong information. This one, entitled Trinity Street, is in fact a view of West Stockwell Street in the Old Dutch Quarter of Colchester. We are looking down from the High Street at the side of the Town Hall. One of the most beautiful domestic buildings in Town stands in the foreground of the picture. Originally part of the Angel Inn, built in 1450. A few years ago it was lovingly restored and is now occupied as offices by a firm of solicitors. Behind the trees also right is Saint Martin's Church and opposite on the left is Saint Martin's Rectory (which can not be seen). There have been great changes here and new skyscraper office blocks of Telecom Limited rise up into into the local skyline or townscape behind Saint Martin's Georgian Rectory, now Telecom offices (1930).

OLD COLCHESTER—STOCKWELL STREET.

35. A close-up of the bottom of West Stockwell Street where it joins or meets 'Stockwell' (a lane). One can behold the previous homes of the Dutch and Flemish weavers. All these buildings are wonderfully preserved. The Colchester Borough Arms are on the left of this 1906 postcard and the Essex County Coat of Arms proudly displayed on the right. There were two public houses opposite each other on this corner of West Stockwell Street. One can just see the Stockwell Arms on the right while left was the Nelson's Head, now a private residence. Jane Taylor, the famous poetess who composed 'Twinkle twinkle little star', once resided in West Stockwell Street. Her house is a tourists delight.

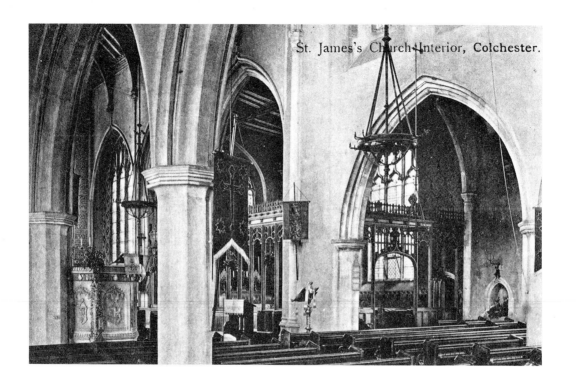

St. James's Church Interior, Colchester.

36. All Saint's Church is in the eastern part of the High Street opposite Castle Park Gates. It has or had a fifteenth century flint tower with a somewhat earlier nave, south aisle and chancel, restored in 1861. They say Colchester 'the Town of Churchs, Inns and Soldiers'. Well, we seem to have a variety of all three. All Saint's became a redundant church some years previously and is now transformed into an interesting Natural History Museum (1902).

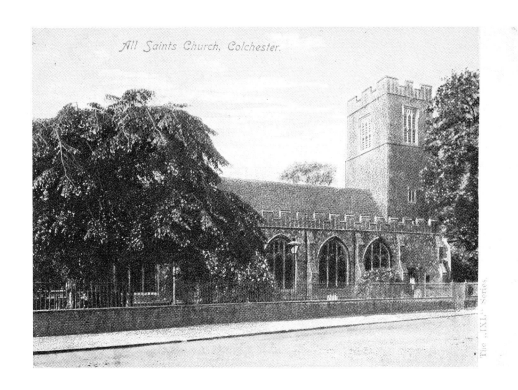

All Saints Church, Colchester.

37. Saint James' Church further along on East Hill is a different kettle of fish and still open for worship in this present age. It was thoroughly restored and partly rebuilt in 1871. There is much Roman brick and brasses to Alderman Maynard, alderman and clothier, and wife 1569 and 1584. There is a local story that Oliver Cromwell held a thanksgiving service here after the Civil War Siege, that he tied his horse up outside to an iron ring that can be viewed to this day (1910).

38. Theatre Royal was situated in Queen Street in 1907. This Street leads off from the junction of East Hill and the High Street. Colchester had many Variety Theatres but Theatre Royal, in the centre of this photograph, was rather special. Erected by the three Nunn brothers in Victoria's reign, it boasted of the D'Oyly Carte Company doing the popular light opera 'H. M. S. Pinafore'. In 1845 Charles Macready played there and other famous stars were Lily Langtry and Gladys Cooper in 1905. There was a dress circle and stalls besides a large number of upper boxes. Also spacious refreshment bars. It was built on the site of a mansion where Edward Clay of Greenstead lived. And near the last old gates of the Town called Saint Botolph's. The Theatre was unfortunately destroyed by fire and today the Police Station and Eastern National Bus Company Garage stand on the site of the old Royal.

39. Saint Botolph's Street is really a continuation of Queen Street as it progresses down to the crossroads or present day roundabout at Saint Botolph's Corner. The ancient monument of Saint Botolph's Priory Church lays in its own grounds behind the busy street. Spoken as the most important ecclesiastical remains in Town. It is even today impressive in its decay. This view of its twelfth century brickwork displays two doorways, seen at the western front, both beautifully moulded. The Priory to which the Church was attached was probably the earliest Augustinian establishment in England. It survived the terrible Dissolution of King Henry VIII because it was also used as a parish Church (1909).

The Priory, Colchester.

40. However like the Music Hall Song of the Edwardian period, in the Civil War it became 'One Of The Ruins That Cromwell Knocked About A Bit'. Being situated just outside the Town Walls and Saint Botolph's Gate, it was sadly used as a target by both Royalists and Roundheads. Norden, the historian, quaintly spelt it as 'Saint Buttulfes in Buttulfe Street'. The huge Norman pillars and grass carpeted Nave are very interesting and cared for by Her Majesties Office Of Works. They stand like glories to the past and are on view to the public at all times (1928).

41. Saint Botolph's Street in 1907. We are looking down the street towards Saint Botolph's Corner and the Mersea Road. The electric tram on the right is going to North Station. Singer's Sewing Machine Shop is on the immediate left, followed by Smiths the Chemists. With its huge pharmaceutical bottles and jars displayed in the shop window. They appeared to be full of coloured water with pharmacy emblems crested in gold. Next to Smiths is Luckings Edwardian Drapery Store, an impressive building of many floors. It had a Lampson compressed air machine that carried customers money in tubes to the high antiquated cash desk, in containers like rockets to the moon. All these premises have now changed hands and only the buildings are left to remind one of there previous use.

42. Saint Botolph's Corner has changed most of all in the last decade. Gone is the Colchester Meat Company Shop on the right and the other shops which included the ancient Plough Inn on the right hand corner. Today a giant roundabout and pedestrian subways link up with the new Southway Bypass on the outskirts of Town (1907).

Colchester, Abbey Gateway,

43. Saint John's Abbey Gatehouse, circa 1906, with the great gates closed. Situated in Saint John's Green near the new modern Southway Bypass which has claimed some of the previous Abbey grounds, and not far from Saint Botolph's, the Gatehouse dates from 1415 and provides an excellent example of flint-panelling. The Eudo Dapifer Governor of Colchester in Norman times founded the Abbey and was buried there. In the twelfth century it became a fine Benedictine establishment where its Abbot wore a mitre and sat in Parliament. At the Dissolution Henry VIII's officers hanged the Abbot John Beche because he refused to hand over the keys of this rich and wealthy Religious House. It was sold or leased to Sir Thomas Darcy (a local man).

S.8063

ST. JOHN'S ABBEY GATE, COLCHESTER

44. Saint John's Abbey Gatehouse in 1928 with the impressive gates open. After the Dissolution the Abbey had various owners and came into the hands of the local Lucas family. All Royalists, who built a fine mansion there using some of the abbey material. During the Great Siege the house was wrecked completely by the Roundheads and in the Gateway high on the vaulted ceiling can be seen the mark made by a cannon ball in that Civil War. After the terrible Siege the Cavalier Sir Charles Lucas was shot by the Parliamentarians. The site of the Abbey is now occupied by the Military and there is an Officers Club in the spacious grounds.

45. Scheregate Steps 1909. These are sited in the Saint John's Street area of Town and thought to be a postern gate opening through the South Roman Wall of Colchester. I recollect little Freddie, a small dwarf man and proper character, selling his winkles and shrimps from the top of Scheregate Steps. In a large wicker-work basket, nearly as big as himself. This rather Dutch style place is still very much tastefully preserved.

Scheregate, Colchester

46. In this delightful wider view of Scheregate a proper artists delight. Taken from the Saint John's Street angle. We can behold the gas lamp-post in the foreground. Gas street lighting arrived in Colchester in 1819. The Steps have always been a useful short cut into Eld Lane, Trinity Street and the Town Centre. Today Scheregate is much more commercialised with a variety of shops. Not far away the new Southway bypass cuts through the Abbeygate Saint John's district. And other signs of recent redevelopment include a tremendous Tescos Supermarket (1908).

47. Head Street like the High Street runs straight in true Roman style within the stout Town Walls. In this scene we are near the North Hill junction glancing down towards the Headgate and crossroads of Saint John, Crouch Street and the Headgate. On the left, just behind the tramwire support pole, is the Fleece Hotel. There is also an entrance to it in Culver Street which is in the foreground left. On the right is Church Street which leads to Saint Mary's. The gabled shop on the corner with the decorative barge boarding dates from 1689 although parts could be much older. Today this is Thorgood's Cakeshop and Restaurant. The high building further along is Colchester Main Victorian Post Office, which has been enlarged quite a few times. In 1897 two houses, a stable and other buildings were demolished to increase its size. Also an entrance was allowed in Church Street for the busy mail carts (1907).

48. The proclamation of the Accession of King George V in 1911 was announced from the Headgate in Head Street. In this scene nearly everyone appears to have turned out to hear the joyful news. From Mayor and Corporation to humble Town policeman. Gill and Son, the high class Photographers on the left, have their front shop blinds respectfully drawn. King George V visited Colchester twice during the Great War to inspect the East Coast defences.

Lexden Church, Colchester.

49. Lexden Church 1910. Lexden was a parish village two miles from Colchester and is now a ward or suburb within the Borough. The Church of Saint Leonard is described as a plain stuccoed building, built in 1820-1821. A new chancel was erected in 1894. I think the Georgian Church has rather a charm of its own with ivy clad walls and unusual cone shaped spire. A considerable amount of earthworks have been discovered at Lexden and not far from the Church is a huge hollow in a wooded area known Lexden Springs. This is referred to as 'King Cole's Kitchen'. But many disbelievers scoff at the mere notion of any culinary operations having ever been carried out on that spot. They say the 'Kitchen' was a Roman Amphitheatre or a gravel pit.

Lexden Road, Colchester.

50. Lexden Road as seen from the Colchester direction going towards the Lexden Church. In the Victorian era Lexden Road became a fashionable promenade for the ladies and gentlemen of the Town. Although they had a Cattle Plague in Lexden village parish in 1866. By 1905, the date of this postcard, the tree lined road was full of select houses and mansions and Lexden was fast becoming a residential suburb of Colchester.

Lexden, near Colchester

51. In this postcard of Lexden, taken from the Colchester side of Lexden Road, there are many historical buildings. The cluster of red roofed houses and cottages on the left are very old, some dating from Tudor and Georgian periods. The one with the wide bay windows is the old ancient Sun Inn. That was there when Lexden was just a pretty village with a 'Blacksmiths Shop'. It has a wealth of oak studs and beams, gleaming brasses and is still a thriving concern. Circa 1910.

LEXDEN STREET, COLCHESTER.

52. A closer view of Lexen Road sometimes called Street. For centuries it has joined up with the London Road. Lexden had a village atmosphere then, as shown here, and the road appears to be partly mud. One can see a section of Saint Leonard's Churchyard wall on the left and one has a good view of the venerable Sun Inn complete with old inn signpost. The Iron Aged fortress city of Cumulodunum covered Lexden and other areas stretching for 12 square miles. Ruled over by Prince Cunobelin, it was the capital of England. Cunobelin had beautiful palaces there and coins minted when other tribes were roaming about in warpaint acting very primitively (1909).

The Bridge, Colchester

53. The Edwardians loved seeing trams photographed in the middle of bridges. It must have been the fashion then for I have discovered many postcards of trams on Colchester's North Bridge. This bridge, erected in Victorian times, was known by the local people as Middleborough because it was near the huge Cattle Market down North Hill. This tram-car appears nearly empty and is advertising Joslins, the local High Street Hardware and Ironmongery Store (1910).

NORTH BRIDGE, COLCHESTER

54. In this view of a rather full up or crowded tram crossing the shallow River Colne we can observe boys fishing on the riverbank. Perhaps these passengers were going or had been to that livestock and deadstock market. The trams ran until 1929 and by then a fleet of buses made these clanking monsters obsolete. They were put on the scrapheap and became backgarden sheds and even caravans (1910).

55. In this 1890 scene of a section showing some of Middleborough Cattle Market we can observe that it was a busy place. Also one can make out the wooden cattle pens filled with sheep and other animals. One could smell the Cattle Market from the top of North Hill on Market Day which was Saturday. A poignant fragrance of beasts from the farmyards being bartered and sold mixed with the aroma of straw or hay. Later the farmers, drovers and buyers entered the New Tavern Public House in the Middleborough Market Place for a well earned pint. Sadly the Tudor tavern (not shown here) was pulled down when the Cattle Market was moved from its traditional site in 1975. Today it is situated up the Severalls Lane area of Colchester in a spanking new building complex away from the town it knew for centuries. Only the name Middleborough is left outside a new Insurance Office Block, but the Marble and Stone drinking fountain has been saved and stands for all to behold the last reminder of that famous Cattle Market.

NORTH STATION ROAD, COLCHESTER

56. In this unusual view, taken from Middleborough Bridge, we are looking down North Station Road. The tram journeying to the North Railway Station will turn round at the Tramway terminus and return to Town via North Hill. The Railway came to Colchester in the 1840's. The Tudor cottage on the left, already mentioned, was at one period a Newsagents Shop and later the 'Copper Kettle Café'. It is now a cafe and boarding house. Those buildings on the right have all disappeared and a new parade of shops fill there former place including an Income Tax Office (1920).

57. On the righthand side of Middleborough's iron bridge, first constructed in 1843, there is a pleasant River Colne walk or footpath going near Middle Mill into Castle Park. This was much favoured by the Edwardians who often promenaded there. Things have now altered over the passing years and on the other side of the River there is a complex of modern office buildings which include a block of offices belonging to the Telecom Limited and the Post Office (1907).

58. Colchester had its share of eccentric characters and the 'Silly Hannahs' became famous in the Town. Often celebrated on picture postcards, these strange figures were sisters, born in 1837. Sometimes also called the 'Two Annahs', they were often seen along the Lexden Road until the turn of the century. One said she was an Indian Princess and the other acted as her maid in waiting and would always walk a few yards behind her sister. They dwelt in Stanwell Street in their earlier lives where they made and sold baskets. But by 1900 they were living on local charity. Eventually one sister died and the remaining one entered the Colchester Workhouse (1902).

59. Jumbo the water-tower stands high on Balkerne Hill, and from ground level to roof apex beyond the tank its height is 131 feet and 5 inches. Jumbo was born or created between 1882 and 1884 at a cost which exceeded £10,000. Nicknamed Jumbo after London Zoos most famous elephant, which was going to America amist national protests for Jumbo had just been sold to Barnums, the American circus proprietor. Jumbo, although not beautiful, is very useful and serves as a balancing reservoir for the Towns early morning water demand. It was the second largest water-tower in England. It had just celebrated its first 100 years and has been listed as a special building of architectural and historic interest (1899).

60. In this Balkerne Lane scene we are glancing down from the Crouch Street direction. The gas lamp on the right is fixed to the rear end of the Horse and Groom Inn. All these buildings have vanished in the last few years. There has been great redevelopment in this area and they even scooped out twenty feet of Balkerne Hill to make the new bypass complete with flyover bridge (1925).

Colchester, St. Mary's Church.

61. Near by the Balkerne Hill Bypass in Church Street is Saint Mary's Church. Known as Saint Mary-at-the-Wall, because there are steps leading to it through a gap in the fine Roman and Norman Town Walls. During the Siege of 1648 it was nearly demolished and almost entirely rebuilt in 1714, with exception of the lower part of the tower (fifteenth century). It was again restored in 1871. During the Great Siege all horses and bridles were brought to Saint Mary's. John Constable considered the tower worthy of his brush and Philip Morant, local historian of Essex, was sometime vicar here. Church Street North leads to Head Street near the General Post Office. Saint Mary's has recently been transformed into a useful Arts Centre for the cultural life of the Town and district (1908).

62. The Balkerne Gateway was the ancient western Roman gateway of Colchester. An inn called 'The Hole In The Wall' now stands upon the site of the northern section of this historical gateway (though its foundations have been thrown open to view). Nothing remains of the big arch which spanned the Roadway, but there remains on the southern side the 'Needle's Eye', used by pedestrians, and the guard-room where Roman sentries dozed in the intervals of outside duty. This little fascinating passage in Balkerne Lane almost beneath Jumbo, the lofty water-tower's eye or trunk, has recently been opened up so that local Colchestrians and tourists can stroll through the Roman Archway and ponder on the power of Imperial Rome. The whole Balkerne Hill area has been much redeveloped and changed with giant multi-storey car parks and the Balkerne Hill Bypass (1930).

63. Crouch Street from the Town end in the Lexden Road direction. The shop near the pony and trap and tramwire support pole on the right is the well established Chemist business of Nunn and Sherry. Very well known in Colchester from about the turn of the century. It was started by William Nunn, a local Councillor. Crouch Street has been cut in half by the new Balkerne Hill Bypass, but still links up with the Lexden Road and eventually the old London Road by going through the Southway. It still has a variety of charming old houses and shops. Like Guntons, which dates back to the Edwardian period and is truly the last old fashion family grocers left in Town. Giving personal specialists service, home cooked hams and a fine selection of quality blended teas and fresh ground coffee (1907).

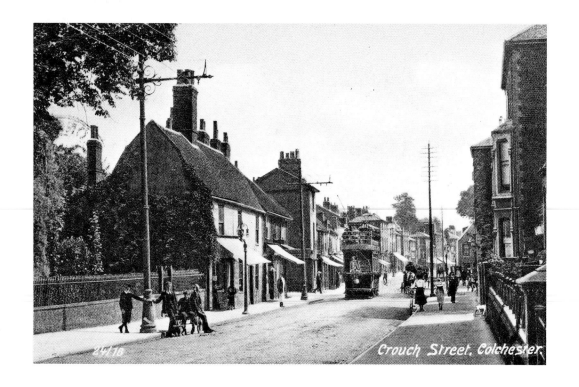

64. Crouch Street in 1906 from the Colchester end of Town showing the section which has been made into a cul-de-sac by the new Balkerne Hill Bypass. The fine Victorian villas on the right have been sacrificed for the bypass. The Essex County Hospital is in the middle distance and the telegraph pole in the background right stands for the communication service of those Edwardian days.

65. Every year about late September time the Mayor, Corporation and some special guests visit the Pyefleet Channel at Mersea Island, a few miles from Colchester. There they sample the oysters accompanied by the traditional gingerbread and gin. This ceremony is a test occasion for the later historical Oyster Feast which takes place in the Town Hall or Castle. In 1930 three million oysters were sold yielding over £26,000. This industry was managed by the Colne Fishery Board and the Colchester Town Council receive a quarter of all profits from the Fishery Board. Today there has been a sad decline in the Oyster trade, but things are improving (1930).

66. Shrub End was a village in Edwardian times and this pretty snow covered scene appears to have all the festive flavour of a Christmas card. All Saint's Victorian Church on the left was built in 1845 and is still in business or use. The Inn sign on the far right is for the Leather Bottle Inn of Tudor origin, which lays further back from view and is still open for trade in this present age. Shrub End, like Lexden, Berechurch, Greenstead and the Hythe and Old Heath, has become suburb of Colchester. A bright star around the big moon of growing Colchester. That is often the fate of pretty villages situated close to spreading towns (1907).

67. Shrub End in 1930 was becoming a busy suburb of Colchester. A place of smart detached houses and bungalows as this picture depicts. Today it is full of private and Council housing estates and seems very much part of Colchester (1930).

Gosbecks Road, Shrub End.

141299

68. Gosbecks Road, Shrub End is not far from All Saint's Church in the Shrub End Road. In this 1930 view we have the picturesque duck pond scene. Gosbecks Road is a very historical Roman site and at Olivers Orchard in 1983, Mr. B. Wade, an Orchard worker, discovered Colchester's largest hoard of Roman coins. He was ploughing a field and found 4,041 bronze content Roman coins in a clay pot, dating from 253-278 A.D. They had laid in the field for 1,700 years undisturbed. Excavations imply that the site had a Roman temple and theatre. They are now awaiting the Treasure Trove inquest on that marvellous discovery (1930).

Canterbury Road School, Colchester.

69. Colchester has a variety of schools. Like Canterbury Road School, many were built at the turn of the century to cater for the growing population. This typical Edwardian building of brick with a red tiled roof, capped by the little bell tower the Edwardians were so fond of incorporating into their seats of learning. The Canterbury Road area is about one mile from Town and full of terraced houses of that same period. It was the new suburb in those days. The school is still teaching the three R's today and the outside complete with railings appears unaltered (1900).

70. Hythe Quay circa 1907 was described in a local guide as 'The Colchester Dockland by the River Colne'. I suppose that description was true as The Hythe is located right of the main Road to Clacton and the East Coast at the foot of the fairly steep East Hill. Colchester's River Colne has always been used for trade and the Romans had a busy port near here called The Old Hythe. After their long occupation it somehow declined and the New Hythe Port was formed and is still in the position. Hythe signifies 'Haven' and in the fifteenth century there was a thriving Fish Market here. Those barges with furled sails would transport wool, grain, coal and even straw or hay. The Common Market has made the East Coast Ports flourishing and Colchester's Hythe is no exception. The Hythe is also known for Davey Paxman and Company, who established the Standard Ironworks in 1876 making boilers. This engineering concern still employs many local Colchestrians.

Old House & Church, Hythe Hill, Colchester. 24.

71. The Hythe was once a village with its own church of Saint Leonard's. The historical square tower can be viewed on the right next to the venerable Tudor cottage which still graces the district. The church dates from the fourteenth century and like the other churches in Colchester suffered much in the Siege. It was also damaged by the earthquake of 1884, but restored again in 1898. Saint Leonard's has just closed after 500 years of service to the local community and they are not sure whether or not to offer the building to the Redundant Churches Fund, who could preserve this ancient structure. This decision could take three years (1915).

HYTHE QUAY, COLCHESTER.

72. The Hythe, as mentioned, was once a village and now forms part of the Borough of Colchester, where it is the chief River Colneside Port. In 1907 the number of vessels registered as belonging to the port was 226. The number of boats and foreign sailing and steam vessels that entered the port that year was 96. There are still many eighteenth century buildings left on the Quay including the Brewery Daniell and Sons, who sold out to Trumans in 1958 (1900).

MILITARY HOSPITAL, COLCHESTER

THE RIFLE RANGE, MIDDLEWICK

73. England was at war with Germany in 1914 and Colchester did her bit for the Great War effort. A series of postcards were printed called 'Doing Our Duty'. This one depicts a view of the Military Hospital in Circular Road and troops having target practice on the local Middlewick Rifle Range. They probably hoped these cards would lift the public morale and show that England was working hard for Victory. In 1917 Colchester had its Great Zeppelin Raid, trams were held up for five hours one evening and bombs fell around the Town. There was an armada of eleven Zeppelins. Some were brought down at nearby places like Old Heath (suburb) and surrounding districts like Tiptree and Wigborough (1914).

74. My uncle Albert from North London joined up in the army. He belonged to a Regiment called the Buff's and was stationed at Colchester for a period during the war before embarking for Flanders. He was one of the lucky soldiers who eventually returned home after four years of conflict in 1918 and married his sweetheart my aunt Ruth. They lived happily ever after. The soldiers lot was fairly hard in the Great War. They had numerous brass buttons and badges to clean in those days. When you signed up they called it 'Taking the Kings Shilling' (1915).

High Street, Colchester

75. During the Great War Colchester had its own Borough Social Club for the troops. Opening in 1914, it was held in the old Public Hall premises in the High Street. This had been the previous Essex and Suffolk Insurance Office, situated near the High Street and North Hill Junction. Wounded troops were entertained at this Social Club with the fine Greek colonnaded appearance. And it provided a place in the centre of Town where soldiers training in the district could spend a pleasant evening. Facilities were provided for writing, reading, games (billiards), chess, draughts etc. Light refreshments, cigarettes, stamps and postal orders were supplied for sale. The Club was free to all men in His Majesty's Forces and stayed open throughout the war (1917).

76. Interior of a Dickinson Hut at the local Essex County General Hospital in Crouch Street. This hospital received wounded soldiers from 1915 and this early pre-fabricated building was named after Mrs. Dickinson, the Hospital commandant, who was later presented with an award 'Member of The British Empire' for her untiring efforts. This type of hut with a centre tortoise stack pipe stove and cast iron beds enabled the hospital to have 250 beds available for the wounded soldiers (1916).

FOR THE HONOUR of COLCHESTER
FEED the GUNS.
OUR GUN WEEK IS NOV. 25th to NOV. 30th

77. Armistice Day the 11th of November 1918. The Mayor, Mr. G. Wright, had only been in office for a few months and now he was standing on the Town Hall balcony with some councillors breaking the joyful news of the Signing of The Armistice. Note the background banner 'Feed The Guns' which was probably asking people to buy War Bonds which would not be needed now as we had made peace with Germany. The crowd must have cheered enthusiastically at this final cessation of hostilities and most appeared to be wearing hats or caps so fashionable in those days. History was being made on that occasion.

78. The Great War Victory Celebrations took place on Sunday the 6th of July 1919. The Mayor, Mr. Wright, made a speech from the Town Hall steps in the crowd filled High Street. There was a march through the Town by the Military and Civilian population. Later a Thanksgiving Service was held in Castle Park which the Mayor and Corporation attended in state. Seen here Mr. Wright outside the Town Hall making his Victory speech (1919).

COLCHESTER WAR MEMORIAL

79. Colchester War Memorial cost over £3,000 to build. It was designed by the sculptor Mr. H.C. Fehr, who had previously done a bust of Victorian Prime Minister Gladstone (of whom Queen Victoria said 'He treats me like a public meeting'). The Statue of Victory in bronze stands 11 feet high. Some shops, cottages and Watts Stoneyard at the eastern end of the High Street were pulled down to make space for the 1914-1918 War Monument and Cowdray memorial gates. They opened up the Castle Park Grounds giving a marvellous view from the High Street angle. Behind the Memorial are the beautiful Cowdray wrought iron gates designed by architect Mr. Duncan Clark. The side gates bear the Crest of the Portreeve of Colchester, while the large middle ones display the arms of the generous Cowdray family. This monument has become a familiar landmark to all (1927).

COLCHESTER, ENTRANCE TO CASTLE PARK

V2300

80. Colchester War Memorial and the Cowdray Gates seen from the Rose Gardens in Castle Park. Watt's Stoneyard, some cottages and shops were demolished in line with this eastern end of the High Street. Although Watt's moved to new premises in Queen Street, which can just be glimpsed through the Memorial Gates (1934).

High Street, Colchester.

81. The High Street shops and inns deserve a special mention. In this busy Edwardian townscape part of the George Hotel can be observed on the near right. Up until 1846 George Samsons Star Stage Coach left the George for Ipswich in Suffolk sharp at 9 o'clock. Further along, by the large projecting lamp, is Mann's Music Shop advertising pianos. It is still selling musical instruments from the same premises. The high building a few doors away by the red tram is the Lamb Hotel, later called The Bay and Say. In 1910, when this postcard was made, there was a fleet of eighteen trams on various routes in the town.

High Street, Colchester

FRITH
CCR 16

82. By 1934 buses were operating all the previous tram routes. One can just be seen on the far right outside the Lamb Hotel. The first bus bought by Colchester Corporation Transport was a single decker 4 Dennis G.S. petrol engine with twenty seats. It was purchased in 1928. On the near right is the George Hotel while on the left is Burstons, the Grocers, and the very well known High Street store of Liptons. Once there was a Liptons in nearly every High Street in England. Now ours has disappeared from the Town, but not from Essex for there is a branch at Clacton-on-Sea on the East Coast. There is a Royal Appointment Sign over this Colchester shop. Sir Thomas Lipton, the Victorian founder of these chain stores, was a yachting friend of King Edward VII. He also employed local Essex men to crew on his racing yachts all named Shamrock. For over fifty years Sir Tommy endeavoured to win for England the America's Cup, but he never fulfilled this ambition (in 1983 the cup was won at last by the Australians).

High Street, Colchester.

83. In 1925 Sainsbury had its Grocery and Provision Store next to the Red Lion Hotel, as shown in the right hand foreground. A place of marble topped counters, brass scales and hand patted butter. Sainsbury's has in the last decade moved into a modern self service supermarket in The Kingsway Shopping Precinct near Queen Street. It also has a new super market outside of Town by the London Road at Lexden. Nextdoor to Sainsbury's is Kendalls, the rainwear and umbrella sellers or stockists, incorporated into the ancient Tudor Red Lion Hotel building. Saint Nicholas' Church makes a good background to this picture. It was restored in 1875/76 by Sir Gilbert Scott and the graceful spire added. He also designed the famous London Albert Memorial near the Albert Hall (1925).

84. In this 1920 view of the High Street looking north we have the Red Lion Hotel on the near left with its centre inner courtyard once used by the stage coaches. The Oyster fishermen would nail up their 'Fish For Sale' notices on the rear Red Lion gateway doors. On the right, behind the ancient steam lorry or waggon, is the Hippodrome Variety Theatre, sometimes called the Grand. This Theatre has for a number of years been a Town Bingo Hall. It has also been a cinema in its varied existence.

85. Colchester Carnival going through the High Street in 1927. This has always been a favourite yearly event and in 1927 £1,660 was raised and given to Colchester's Essex County Hospital. There appears to be some Ancient Britons here and Chinese Coolies. The Carnival is still held each year and local firms and shops put on a colourful display of floats raising more funds for charity (1927).

Town Hall, Colchester

86. In this portrait of the Town Hall, taken in 1917, we can see the handsome red brick 'Cup's Hotel adjoining the High Street Town Hall. The Cup's had an elegant rear Assembly Room dating from 1795. In 1801 Lord Nelson of Trafalgar reknown called there for refreshments on his journey through Colchester. And in November that year the exiled King of France, Louis XVIII, with attendants gathered in the splendid 'New Room' open for reception of Royal guests. By 1819 it was classed as one of the finest inns of England.

87. In this majestic study of the Town Hall we can observe part of the opulent Cup's Hotel on the left. The Assembly Room and Minstrels Gallery were demolished in 1965 and the whole hotel was eventually pulled down in 1972. A modern four storey block of shops and offices now takes up its former position. At the moment the old Cup's Hotel sign of three golden cups swings majestically outside the new Cup's Inn down Trinity Street, not a stones throw away from the High Street (1904).

CHR 24 THE RED LION HOTEL, COLCHESTER A TUCK CARD

88. This postcard of 1936 could be entitled 'Market Day' in the High Street outside the Red Lion Hotel. Kendall and Sons Limited are advertising 'Sunshades and Umbrellas' over their shop window on the right while next-door J. Sainsbury has a Royal Appointment sign over his store. Sainsbury's have now moved to the Kingsway, as previously mentioned, and a big Marks and Spencer Superstore stands on their old site. The Red Lion still has its centre archway and courtyard with fascinating timber studs and fine sixteenth century carved panels. Now you walk through the archway into a modern shopping complex. The Market has returned to the High Street after many years.

M2361 SILVER QUEEN Buses in Colchester c1921
(Lamb Hotel)

Pamlin Prints
Croydon

89. Although Colchester was served by trams until 1929, buses did journey through the Town from other areas. Notably the Silver Queen buses which were solid tyred, open roofed conveyances and petrol driven they came from East Coast Seaside places like Clacton and Walton. These two are in the High Street near the Lamb Hotel not far from the Town Hall (1921).

HIGH STREET LOOKING WEST, COLCHESTER.

21500

90. The High Street in 1936 showed a few changes to the curious eye. The era of the trams was long past and accounts for the vanished tramlines and overhead wires. The tram-wire poles seemed to have been conveniently adapted to take electric street lighting as the one on the left proves. Cars are parked on both sides of the street like the pattern of modern day things. The George Hotel on the near right complete with porter seems to be doing a thriving business. Advertising 'Restaurant', 'Luncheons' and 'Teas'.

91. Neal and Robarts high quality Cake shop and Tea rooms stood in the High Street at number 11B during the 1930's and many years afterwards. The premises were not far from the Town Hall, but on the opposite side. The proprietors were two maidenly ladies and their speciality was homemade cakes, especially Seed Cake.

92. Neal and Robarts had some most unusual wall panel paintings in their front Tea Rooms which overlooked the busy High Street. The house, now a shop, was very old (probably Queen Anne or Georgian) and they had discovered the wall paintings in a rear room which they wanted to transform into a kitchen. They had them rehung in the Café Room, but on their retirement the historical oil paintings were taken down. Some found a new home at the Castle Museum and others, less fortunate, were put on the rubbish heap (1930).

93. They were very proud at Neal and Robarts Tea Rooms of their cellar Café. They walls were made of real genuine Roman bricks. So the Romans had left their stamp on Colchester which had lasted for more than 1900 years (1930).

94. In this study of Trinity Street we are looking towards Culver Street. Behind in the background is the Victoria Clock Tower of the High Street Town Hall. Holy Trinity Church is famed far and wide for its Saxon tower and in particular for its small arrow-head doorway in the western face. There is a monument with long Latin inscription to the justly celebrated William Gilberd, the father of the modern science of electricity. He was born in this parish in 1540 and died in 1603. Holy Trinity became empty and derelict for a number of years. The nightly home of local tramps and down and outs. Fortunately it was rescued in the 1970's and is at present a Rural Crafts Museum (1907).

95. The Saxon arrow-head doorway of Holy Trinity seems very useful as a noticeboard. In this close-up picture one can behold the Roman tiles re-used between the brickwork. There had been great redevelopment in this area in the previous few years. There is a modern square called Trinity and the Public Library besides the new Lion Walk and Culver Street Shopping Precinct (1907).

Hyderabad Barracks, Colchester

96. Colchester has been a Garrison Town since the Roman occupation and these troops training at Hyderabad Barracks in 1916 was not an unusual sight. In the Napoleonic Wars the soldiers camped out in tents in the Abbey Fields, once belonging to Saint John's Abbey, and in the Mersea Road direction out of Town. By the nineteenth century the Military looked apon Colchester as one of their permanent camps. In the Crimean War of 1855 wooden pre-fab huts were built at Hyderabad and Abbey Fields. They were supposed to last only ten years, but were not replaced with brick barracks until 1900. The brick barracks, seen here on the left, have been modernised in recent years.

Officers' Mess, Hyderabad Barracks, Colchester

76386.(J.V)

97. The Officers Mess at Hyderabad in 1928. There are many Army Barracks within the Borough with names like Cateau, Kinkee, Goojerat and Cavalry. Also a big Military Corrective Camp Establishment at Berechurch Hall (a ward or suburb of town). In 1856 Prince Albert visited the new wooden Army Camps and crowds gave him a loyal welcome. About one thousand flags flew over North Hill, Head, High Street and Queen Street.

Military Hospital, Colchester

98. The Military Hospital, built in 1896, is in the Circular Road surrounded by the barracks just mentioned. It has always served the local population although it is really an Army Hospital. Colchester mothers often had their babies there, but now it is only partly open for Army Personnel (1927). Now there are plans to close the hospital altogether and make it into the Eastern Divisional Headquarters of the Military.

99. There have been major redevelopments in Culver Street, which was more or less a back lane to the High Street. Now it has been cut in half by the new shopping complex and called West and East Culver Street. In this study we are looking along the western section towards Head Street. On the left is the huge building of The Fleece Hotel, once so popular with the Commercial Travellers or Salesmen. It was demolished in 1970. The Tudor Café by the narrow bottleneck entry for Culver Street was always a traffic hazard and was cleared away in the 1940's (1930).

100. The Corporation Fire Brigade was formed in 1896 and here they stand proudly by their fire engine outside Colchester Castle. In 1879 they had the volunteer brigade, but this was later disbanded and their engine taken over by Colchester Corporation. Earlier the Town had a fire service managed by the Suffolk Equiable Insurance Society, who had the expense of inspecting and testing the four manual engines, which had previously been the responsibility of the church wardens of Saint Peter's, All Saint's, Holy Trinity and Saint James' parishes (1896).

101. A snowscape of Sheepen Bridge and Road, taken in 1902. Then it was little more than a narrow lane that stretched from Lexden to the Middleborough Cattle Market in North Hill. Sheepen Farm in the background right has now disappeared and the wooden bridge over the River Colne has been replaced. The lane has been transformed into a modern road to cater for the present day traffic. Once farmers drove their flocks of sheep along Sheepen Road to the Sheep- pens of the North Hill Cattle Market. (Perhaps that is how it got that unusual name.) Today there is a nursery, Technical College, and school named Saint Helena along Sheepen Road and a big roundabout where it joins the Balkerne Hill Bypass.

Colchester.   Middle Mill.

The Wrench Series, No. 9401

102. Colchester once had many water-mills and Middle Mill stood by the River Colne on the ground which is now part of Castle Park. Sometimes known as Chopping's Mill, because a family of that name owned it and lived there for a number of years. The artatched miller's house left looks quite big and roomy and in the distance left can be seen Saint Peter's Church Tower. In 1863 2,000 spectators watched an exciting boat race. The two boats raced from North Bridge (Middleborough) to Middle Mill and back. In the winter there was also skating on the river by the old mill. The Town had many wind corn-mills and several water-mills in 1840 (1902).

Middle Mill, Colchester.

103. Mills were very important to the ancient life of Colchester and all seemed to have been situated outside the Town Walls. Middle Hill was in Castle Park beyond the huge Roman Wall by the River Colne. It was demolished after the Second World War in the 1950's. There is a local tale that in times of Siege a bell would ring out its warning from the walled Town of Colchester and all the millers from their various mills would come to seek the shelter and safety of those stout Town Walls. There were many mills around the Town including Marriages, already mentioned, Cannock and Bourne Mill. These are still standing (1907).

Old Bourne Mill, COLCHESTER.

104. Another such mill was the picturesque Bourne Mill, which is now National Trust property and open to the public on certain days at a modest fee. They think that after the Dissolution of Saint John's Abbey some of the stones were used in the construction of the pretty little Bourne Mill lying about ¾ of a mile south-east of the Abbey Gateway. The Mill, a dainty work with elaborate gables, treated in the Dutch manner so common in Essex. A small tablet states 'Thomas Lucas 1591'. (He owned Saint John's Abbey property after the Dissolution period.) A picture from 1909.

105. An unusual study of Bourne Mill from the rear. Here we can see the weather-boarded projecting upper storey which held the hoist. This was a water-mill with a pond at the front. It had enormous mill-stones to grind the grain into flour which was probably collected by horse and cart as was the custom. Bourne Mill was a proper working mill, not a pretty little fishing lodge as stated in some Essex Guides. Although they probably fished in the Mill Pond on occasions (1907).

106. This 1927 picture of a tram crossing East Bridge reveals three stories. On the left is Marriages Flour Mill, established in 1840. Today this has been much renovated and is now the Mill Hotel. Marriages have transfered their business to the Cowdray Avenue Industrial Centre on the North Station side of town. They are still advertising themselves as 'The Master Millers'. Between 1927 and 1928 East Bridge was reconstructed and the dangerous middle hump removed. This tram is probably one of the last ones to cross the bridge for they never replaced the tramlines or rails and in 1928 trams on this East Gates route were replaced with two new bus services.

107. The Town Walls of Colchester have been extensively repaired at least twice, but are still fundamentally a Roman work. Ten feet thick and re-inforced on all sides by stout earthen embankments, the walls were nigh unbreachable. Roads follow the course of the walls around the Town and in Castle Park a public footpath leads across the massive wall. After the Great Siege General Fairfax, the Roundhead leader, commanded that the fortifications be lowered by a few feet. 'Never again', he said, 'shall this town be forced to stand against its Parliament.' Once there were five main gateways into Colchester, the Head, North Balkerne and not over-looking East and Saint Botolph's Gate. Now only the early Roman ruin of Balkerne remains (1910).

COLCHESTER.
BASTION ON ROMAN WALL

108. A fleet of Trojan vans, perhaps the first in Colchester, were sold by Captain Baker, who opened a garage enterprise in Queen Street in 1922. In 1925, the date of this picture, vans had been sold to local T.R. Blake, milkman, E.G. Sach, High Street Grocer, and even to a Mr. A.J. Mason from far away: Walton-on-the-Naze by the East Coast (1925).